The Monster Outside My Door

Story by
Timothy M. Cordes

Cover Illustration
Ruthann Cordes Baker

Interior Design and Illustrations
Timothy M. Cordes   Justine Babcock

Dedication

To children both young and old
who face their fears every day

There is a monster outside my door.

Not in the closet, or under the floor.
All covered with hair and a big pointy snout.
He waits outside til I come out,
This monster outside my door...

Not all monsters are the same,
Some are meek and mild and tame.
Sometimes He is big or very small,
Sometimes he is wide or very tall,
This monster outside my door...

He follows me wherever I go.
From home, to school...

...or the picture show.
Sometimes he laughs and sometimes he
cries.
Even though he is ten feet high,
This monster outside my door...

He walks with me stride for stride,
To the doctor's office he is by my side.

He scares me most when I'm lying there,
Waiting and waiting in my dentist chair,
This monster outside my door...

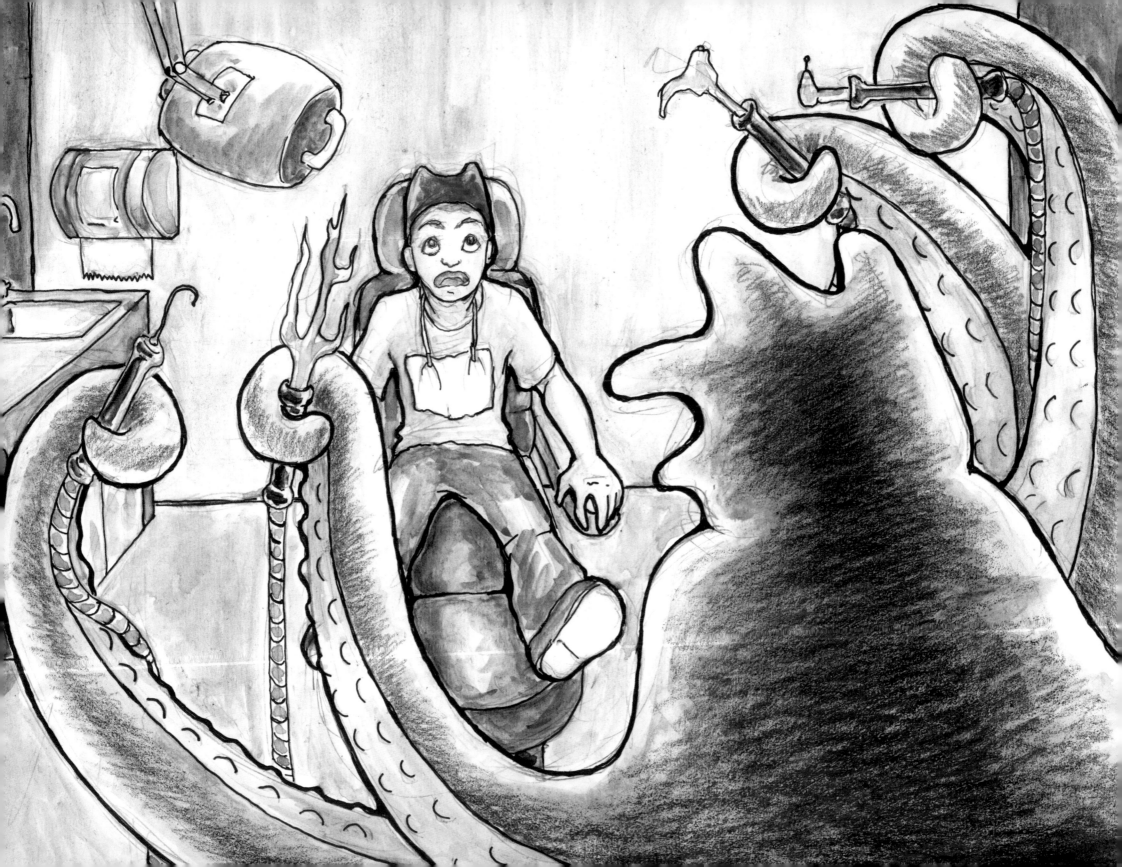

He gets so big, as big as a boulder,
He gets so heavy when he sits on my
shoulder.
If he is this big now, what will he be when
I'm older?
This monster outside my door...

We all have a monster outside our door,
But is this monster really a monster at
all?

Or just the world outside our door?

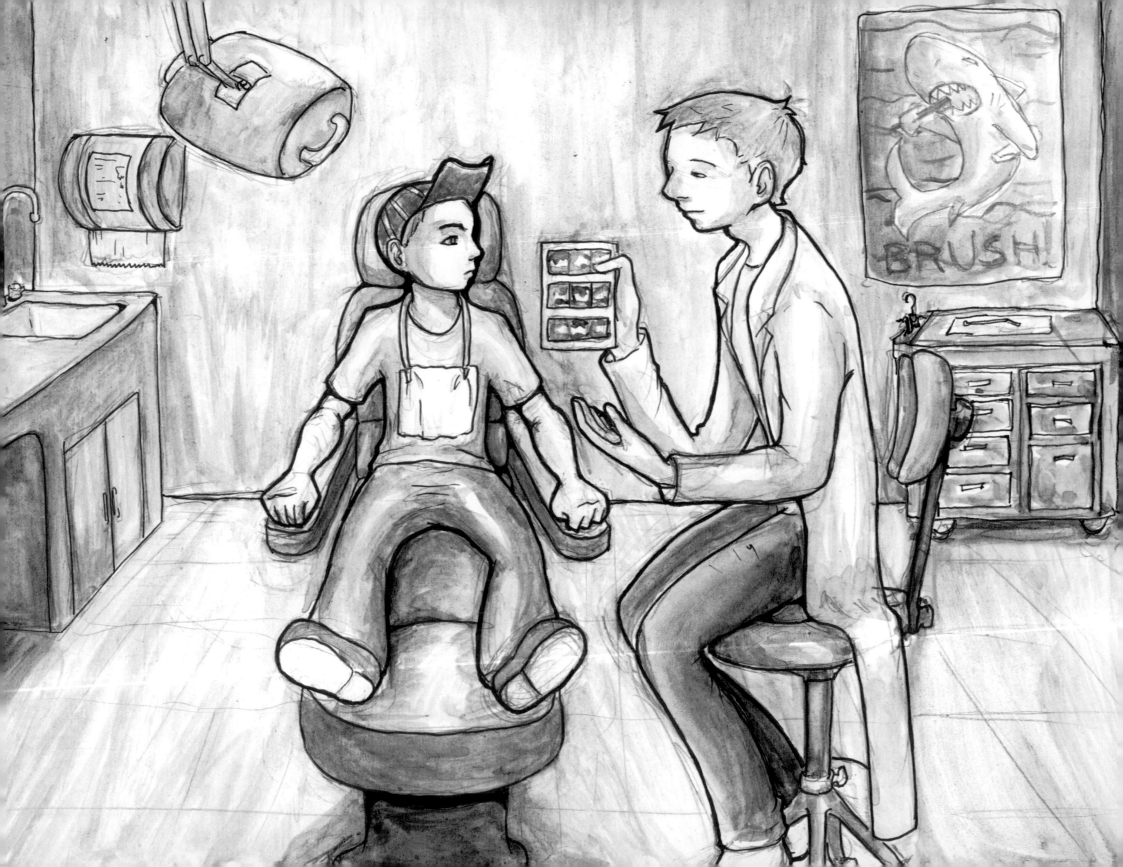

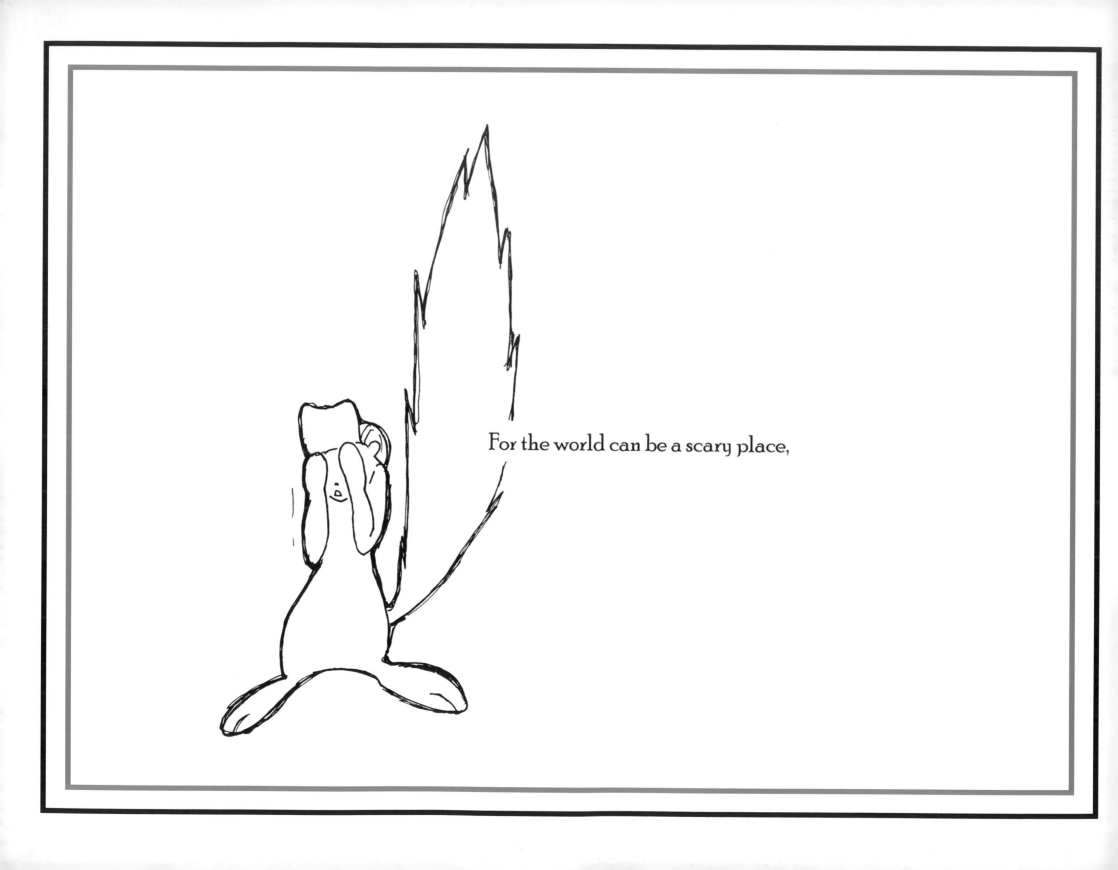

For the world can be a scary place,

And sometimes wears a monster's face.

He could be a monster that's good and
kind,
If only we leave our fears behind.
As we grow and see the light,
Of beautiful days all sunny and bright,
This monster that we fear and dread,
Will slowly pass and bow his head.

So don't be afraid of the monsters you see,
For after all it is you and me.
Be good and kind and help others to
grow,
And even take in a picture show.

The End

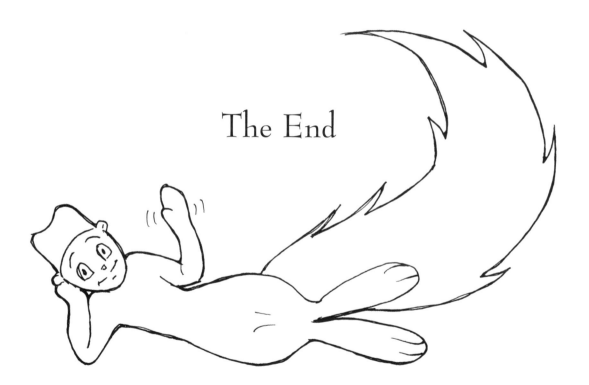